FEB **22** 2018

P9-CLI-266

COOL COMPETITIONS

*Incredible*

# DRONE
# COMPETITIONS

BY THOMAS K. ADAMSON

CAPSTONE PRESS
a capstone imprint

Blazers Books are published by Capstone Press,
1710 Roe Crest Drive, North Mankato, Minnesota 56003
www.mycapstone.com

Copyright © 2018 by Capstone Press, a Capstone imprint. All rights reserved.
No part of this publication may be reproduced in whole or in part, or stored
in a retrieval system, or transmitted in any form or by any means, electronic,
mechanical, photocopying, recording, or otherwise, without written permission
of the publisher.

**Library of Congress Cataloging-in-Publication Data**
Names: Adamson, Thomas K., 1970– author.
Title: Incredible drone competitions / by Thomas K. Adamson.
Description: Mankato, Minnesota : Capstone Press, [2018] |
  Series: Blazers. Cool competitions | Audience: Age 8–12. |
  Audience: Grade 4 to 6. | Includes bibliographical references and index.
Identifiers: LCCN 2017002063 (print) | LCCN 2017003676 (ebook) |
  ISBN 9781515773542 (library binding) | ISBN 9781515773580 (eBook PDF)
Subjects: LCSH: Airplane racing—Juvenile literature. | Drone aircraft—
  Juvenile literature.
Classification: LCC GV759 .A33 2018 (print) | LCC GV759 (ebook) |
  DDC 797.5/2—dc23
LC record available at https://lccn.loc.gov/2017002063

**Editorial Credits**
Aaron Sautter, editor; Kyle Grenz, designer; Eric Gohl, media researcher;
Steve Walker, production specialist

**Photo Credits**
Alamy: David Stock, 7, 8, 25, 26–27, 29; AP Photo: Nick Ut, 22; Getty Images:
Anadolu Agency, 21, Drew Angerer, 18, Sean Gallup, 17; Newscom: picture-
alliance/dpa/Jan Woitas, 11; Shutterstock: Absemetov, cover (bottom),
aerogondo2, 15, Jag_cz, 5, The Polovinkin, cover (top), Tochanchai, 12

Printed and bound in China.
0517/CA21700460 042017 004883

# TABLE OF CONTENTS ▶

# A NEW WAY TO FLY

▶ Drones give pilots an exciting way to fly. These **remote-controlled** aircraft fly in ways that few vehicles can. Many people fly drones just for fun. But some people compete in serious drone contests around the world.

**remote-controlled**—controlled from a distance; remote-controlled aircraft are flown by pilots using a controller on the ground

# INCREDIBLE COMPETITIONS

▶ The world's best drone pilots compete in races, **freestyle**, and combat events. Some large events give away big cash prizes to winning **contestants**.

**freestyle**—a type of competition in which contestants are free to use various tricks and moves

**contestant**—a person who takes part in a competition

**FACT**

During night-time races, LED lights on drones make them easier to spot. Race courses are also often marked with neon lights.

## FACT

Racing drones can travel up to
75 miles (121 kilometers) per hour.
Some are even faster!

Pilots race drones through tough courses. They don't just turn left and right. They also go over, under, and through **obstacles**. Most events take place outdoors. Some events are held in large stadiums or empty buildings.

**obstacle**—an object or barrier that competitors must avoid during a race

# HIGH-TECH FLYING

▶ Many pilots compete with **quadcopter** drones. Pilots often use first-person-view (FPV) goggles. These goggles allow the pilot to see what the drone "sees". It's like playing a video game in real life.

**quadcopter**—a drone that uses four rotors to fly

## FACT

Professional FPV goggles often cost between $200 and $600.

camera

**FACT**

Competition drones are often made of
lightweight **carbon fiber**. The tough
frames can handle crashes.

Most competitive drones have **high-definition** cameras. The cameras help pilots see where drones are going during a race. Cameras also give fans a great view on TV and computer screens!

**high definition**—technology that displays videos or pictures with a very sharp, clear image

**carbon fiber**—a strong, lightweight material made of very thin threads of carbon

A pilot's remote control sends radio signals to the drone. Another signal links the drone and the pilot's FPV goggles. The radio signals use different **frequencies** so they don't get mixed up.

**frequency**—the number of sound waves that pass a location in a certain amount of time

# FACT

Remote controls for most drones have a range of about 0.5 mile (0.8 km). Some can work as far away as 3.7 miles (6 km).

# DRONE BATTLES AND FREESTYLE

▶ Drone combat is like a boxing match. Pilots try to knock one another's drones out of the air. Drone combat is a test of tough drone design. Many pilots build or **modify** their drones for these events.

**modify**—to change or alter in some way

FACT

The Aerial Sports League started a drone combat event called Game of Drones in 2013.

Pilots test their flying skills in freestyle competitions. Their drones do mid-air flips and spins to earn points. They may do tricks around obstacles or fly very close to the water.

FACT

One freestyle trick is called the corkscrew. A drone flies in twisting circles around a bridge as it moves along the length of it.

# CHAMPIONSHIP RACING

▶ In some drone races, pilots go through qualifying **heats**. Pilots with the best times move to the **elimination** rounds. The winners keep moving up until someone wins the championship.

**heat**—one of several early races that determine which competitors advance to the main event

**elimination**—removed from competition by losing

2016 Paris Drone Festival in Paris, France

FACT

The first U.S. National Drone Championships were held in California in 2015.

In the Drone Racing League, pilots earn points during the racing season. Those with the most points can compete in the World Championship race.

FACT

Pilots in the Drone Racing League all use the same type of drone. Only the most skilled pilot wins the race.

The first ever World Drone Prix took place in 2016. It was held in Dubai, United Arab Emirates. The pilots raced drones through brightly lit gates and other obstacles.

FACT

The World Drone Prix also included a twisting "joker lane". Pilots had to follow this special part of the course at least once during the race.

World Drone Prix race course in Dubai, United Arab Emirates

25

Drone Worlds took place in Hawaii in 2016. It was the world's largest drone competition. Pilots came from more than 30 countries. They competed in both racing and freestyle contests.

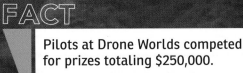

FACT

Pilots at Drone Worlds competed for prizes totaling $250,000.

Drone pilots compete for major awards. At the World Drone Prix, pilots were awarded prizes totalling $1 million. Skilled drone pilots will keep competing to be the best!

England's Luke Bannister (right) won the top prize at the 2016 World Drone Prix in Dubai. The 15-year-old pilot won $250,000.

# Glossary

**carbon fiber** (KAHR-buhn FY-buhr)—a strong, lightweight material made of very thin threads of carbon

**contestant** (kuhn-TES-tuhnt)—a person who takes part in a competition

**elimination** (i-li-muh-NAY-shuhn)—removed from competition by losing

**freestyle** (FREE-styl)—a type of competition in which competitors are free to use various tricks and moves

**frequency** (FREE-kwuhn-see)—the number of sound waves that pass a location in a certain amount of time

**heat** (HEET)—one of several early races that determine which competitors advance to the main event

**high definition** (HYE def-uh-NISH-uhn)—technology that displays videos or pictures with a very sharp, clear image

**modify** (MOD-ih-fye)—to change or alter in some way

**obstacle** (OB-stuh-kuhl)—an object or barrier that competitors must avoid during a race

**quadcopter** (KWAHD-cop-tuhr)—a drone that uses four rotors to fly

**remote-controlled** (ri-MOHT-kuhn-TROHLD)—controlled from a distance; remote-controlled aircraft are flown by pilots using a controller on the ground

# Read More

**Chandler, Matt.** *Recreational Drones.* North Mankato, Minn.: Capstone Press, 2017.

**Faust, Daniel R.** *Entertainment Drones.* New York: PowerKids Press, 2016.

**Hustad, Douglas.** *Discover Drones.* Minneapolis: Lerner, 2016.

**Marsico, Katie**. *Drones.* New York: Children's Press, 2016.

# Internet Sites

Use FactHound to find Internet sites related to this book.

Visit *www.facthound.com*

Just type in 9781515773542 and go.

Super-cool stuff!

Check out projects, games and lots more at
**www.capstonekids.com**

# Index

Simsbury Public Library
Children's Room